Icon and Evidence

ICON *and* EVIDENCE

poems

MARGARET GIBSON

 Louisiana State University Press
Baton Rouge

2001

Copyright © 1973, 1986, 1998, 1999, 2000, 2001 by Margaret Gibson
All rights reserved
Manufactured in the United States of America
First printing
10 09 08 07 06 05 04 03 02 01
5 4 3 2 1

Designer: Amanda McDonald Scallan
Typeface: Sabon
Printer and binder: Thomson-Shore, Inc.

Library of Congress Cataloging-in-Publication Data

Gibson, Margaret.
   Icon and evidence : poems / Margaret Gibson.
   p. cm.
   ISBN 0-8071-2709-4 (cloth : alk. paper) — ISBN 0-8071-2710-8 (pbk. : alk. paper)
   I. Title.

PS3557.I1916 I28 2001
813'.54—dc21
                                                                                       2001029892

The author gratefully acknowledges the editors of the following publications, in which the poems listed first appeared, sometimes in slightly different form: *Arts and Letters:* "Amaryllis," "In the Heart of the Mountains," "Requiem: A Poem in Five Voices"; *Five Points:* "Elegy in Soviet Georgia," "Listening to Ramón"; *Freshwater:* "Postcards in March"; *Georgia Review:* "The Funeral," "Icon" ("To raise her spirits"), "Mango"; *Gettysburg Review:* "Epistle to Gerard Manley Hopkins," "House of Stone and Song," "Practice for a Requiem," "Strange Altars"; *Hampden Sydney Poetry Review:* "Icon" (*"That man standing there"*); *Hubbub:* "Elegy for a Dancer"; *Image:* "Icon" (*"Let whoever is sinless"*); *Iowa Review:* "Archaeology," "Icon" (*" Thou still unravished—"*); *Kenyon Review:* "Deep Water"; *New England Review:* "Hymn to Night"; *New Virginia Review:* "White Iris, Old Memory"; *The Recorder:* "At Dún Dúchathair"; *Seneca Review:* "Primary Reflections: After Reading the Children's First Letters to God"; *Sewanee Review:* "Collect" ("In strict abundance"), "Collect" ("Just now in the living room"), "Comet"; *Shenandoah:* "Skunk Cabbage"; *64:* "Iona Canticle," "Pilgrimage"; *Southern Review:* "Epistle to Robinson Jeffers," "Epistle to the Field in Eldred, Pennsylvania"; *West Branch:* "Compline" (If, as we say, it's true"), "Compline" ("In the time of night prayer").

"Archaeology" was awarded a Pushcart Prize and was reprinted in *Pushcart Prize XXVI: Best of the Small Presses.*

"Epistle to the Field in Eldred, Pennsylvania" was awarded honorable mention in the 2000 Robinson Jeffers Tor House Prize for Poetry.

The author is grateful to the University of Connecticut for a faculty research travel grant that made possible a journey to the Isle of Iona off the coast of Scotland.

The paper in this book meets the guidelines for permanence and durability of the Committee on Production Guidelines for Book Longevity of the Council on Library Resources. ∞

This book is for my sister Elizabeth

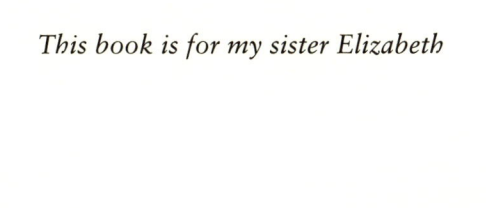

CONTENTS

Canticle

    Comet / 3
    Collect / 5
    Epistle to Gerard Manley Hopkins / 6
    Amaryllis / 9
    Skunk Cabbage / 11
    Postcards in March / 13
    Iona Canticle / 16
    House of Stone and Song / 19
    Icon / 24

Complaint

    Icon / 29
    In the Heart of the Mountains / 31
    Listening to Ramón / 33
    Elegy in Soviet Georgia / 37
    Elegy for a Dancer / 40
    Primary Reflections: After Reading the
        Children's First Letters to God / 43

Collect / 46
Epistle to Robinson Jeffers / 47
Archaeology / 50

Confession

Practice for a Requiem / 53
White Iris, Old Memory / 55
The Funeral / 57
Deep Water / 58
Mango / 59
Icon / 61
Collect / 67
Epistle to the Field in Eldred, Pennsylvania / 68

Compline

Compline / 73
Pilgrimage / 74
Strange Altars / 75
At Dún Dúchathair / 77
Compline / 82
Requiem: A Poem in Five Voices / 83
Collect / 89
Epistle for January 19, 1999 / 90
Tenebrae / 92
Icon / 96
Compline / 99
Night-Blooming Cereus / 100
Hymn to Night / 102

Notes

Canticle

From its haunt within the mountain, what's hidden calls out.
Star fire. A moon of hazy milk. What more do I want?

COMET

I wait until last light opens
        into an obedient listening,
    a reverie that includes the rapt attention
of the moon, and the pickerel frogs
        hard at their vesper canons,
    their singing given out with such
jubilant abandon, I sense
        the pond, the road,
    even the candent lapis of the evening sky
as forms of their strange joy.

When finally it's time, I walk
        the lane of swamp maples and oaks
    and come into the damp, open fields—
and there it is, looking for all the world
        as if someone
    opened a window up there,
the blurred light of heaven roving out.
        An annunciation?
    I hear only its plangent silence. It requires
nothing. Awaits nothing. Asks nothing.

I could continue to call it *porthole, angel,*
        herald—or refuse to,
    an apophatic reprieve,
its funereal wake of ice and debris all I see,
        and gauze at that.
    Given the distance, how can I
know what to make of its thunder and furnace,
        its burly habit of blazing—
    a succession of lucidities so vast,
any sensible humility would catch its breath.

But dear God, all I want is to be here,
        my tiny anguish and my joy
    a moment's notice, an equivalent cry
just as two Canadas
        honk a path across the dark fields,
   flying lower than the rim of the long stone wall,
lower than the wetland rushes,
        all the gramarye and splendor
   of this wide and terrible plenitude somehow
intermingled with their sudden, ragged and ridden, litany.

COLLECT

Full of itself for hours, now wind falls away.

From walking the bottomland
I come up the low rise
                just ahead of the last

sweep of shadow down the field—

the sun's whole round
and the sticks of the winter rose bush

meet—the breast of a bird on its nest,
hollowing.
          Flaring its wings.

EPISTLE TO GERARD MANLEY HOPKINS

After clarity and eclipse, this morning
dawn's a straight blue stroke, low clouds
of watershed and lazulite blue, skylark
layers of near tone, unrolling long, like waves
on the shallowing shore, edge to unraveled
edge as steady as the flow of distant hills.
Like you, I like to look at things.
By solitary revel, solitude's made
more wakeful, *carved and scuppled* as you said
of a snow field whose ridges spread out
in flinty waves, relief maps and the grain
of wood ensculpted there, lawed in by wind
that rippled the roadside sallows you redeemed
by noting their color, *ginger, road rut*, words
I borrow now for the winter beech leaves,
their fitful quaking in quick wind just
my mood, I don't know why. And I wonder
at the restraint of your taut vocation,
the fell of dark, not day your sometimes cloister—
Oh, but the roister of clouds, the threshing flail
of syllables, mute spires in blue haze,
panicles of orchis, bluebell bridges of swooping
swallows, tinges, voluptuous fringes—
these flared for you, flowed, showed you . . . what?
You said you wore the wind, braids of it, folds
and skirls, like light linen, your own body
needed to *thew and fire and blood it in,*
just as wind needs a flag, or as winding current,
made subtle in deep clear pools, requires
green supple cresses, else we cannot see it.
Last night I watched earth's shadow scale the moon,
a fumbled blur at the lower rim at first,
the line that firms the form unsure, then erasure—
and no strophic cry from the barred owl
to mark the moment. I understood *occlude*,

earth the cloud that blocks the sun, *cloud
as hill*, homologous down to its old English
root, *clud* akin to *clod*. But a low gauze
of actual cloud slurred in from the west and glazed
the sky, the diminished moon more luminous thereby.
Against that veil the branches of the oak
stood out, more clearly there—then sharply not
as the veil rent, and the moon went darker.
The shadow that welled below the bowl of flowers
on the sill went shallow, and Hopkins,
it was then I took my vow, to just what
I do not know, as you did to God—
I took my vow, you wrote in your notebook,
that one day's entry four bald words, no
reckoning up, no rinsing thrill of trumpet,
no splay of vine. No ash, no elm, no keel
in the ruddy tumult, no sponging out
of the damask hills by rain, no northern lights.
Thus it was you gave yourself, entirely dark,
without comment or end punctuation . . .
but just as I am writing *entirely dark*
a dull thump at the window, muffled,
strikes me still, unlatches then catches me
swift to the sill, where, down from the oak
shearing over, or from the shagbark swept
too near, a bird has flown into itself,
in the unfathomed depth of the selfless glass
its own self-shadow seen too late—too late
in the riddling and (your word) *fire dint* rise
and fall of bright air and curved branch—rebuffed,
then stunned, or worse. Too firmly I hold
to what I've seen before, expecting to find
a smudge, a smear, *blear share* and bits of down,
a hint of blood. But there on the glass,
foreshortened, the whole bird, ghosted, is—
its shrugged head sidewise, soft breast full on,
plush, the arc of its extended wing, the front edge
of its flying there, obliquely, as if
with a soft brush a Taoist had summoned

from ink and water, as gracefully awry
as the fling of early forsythia,
the essence of grief—for it is a mourning dove,
I think, windhovering, backlit by bright air,
Chriosd—the look of the word in Gaelic very like
your savior, but smudged, dredged up unwanted,
the blunt breath of that moment of impact
held on the glass, and so breathtaking, so
beautiful I can tell the flash and mortal
dazzle of the bird, and its probable pain—
mind-sloggering, smoldered and unadorned
auras of invisible pain. No need
to ask you, Hopkins, what works so darkly
in our favor, and sustains. What keeps me
from blank despair is just this word-tumbled
world of ours, not ours, rough not rounded,
scabrous not smooth, pitted, pocked and twisted,
twined, twinned, all its pattern and disturbance
evidence of power, *poisèd power*,
entirely dark, flung at random toward us,
or wrung out of us, ready or not—ours
only to give, obliquely faithful, back. And so
you said lavish, or little; you looked, and your soul,
entirely dark, impoverished, chaste, sent back
in song your unborn, deathless self—that is,
everything and nothing, like the moon eclipsed
in fullest meeting. And the dove? I found no dove
on the hard ground. I missed the moment it cleared
the glass and veered off, unsteady, into the upsoaring wind.
And then, like grace the rain, the rain misting in.

AMARYLLIS

God in the near
onion, in the wintered song sparrow
in the long-gone scarlet tanagers, God in the school of orange
carp and the dark amber of watery
weeds, God
in the tissue of chaste berry and skullcap—
God, I have been looking for you
months of waiting
since the last flamboyant flame of leafing
on the worn-down
amaryllis
whose seven red trumpets
could have blown down the walls of Jericho
and raised up the rubble
had I known how to play them
had I known how to let
them play me—
God in the up-welling
phase of green reeds, ungainly God
a strut of green
from the bulb, like a cockscomb
God in the last green flare left
to thirst in the sun,
the arc and graceful swoop of it
the startled brow of the invisible
all-seeing
eye of the boundless—
God in the bulb, God in the faceless dark
this morning my hands
lift you
scaly and dry, squat, used as you are to the ease
of unlit corners in the cool closet where
winter apples and oranges
ember—

God, I give you back to the bonfire sun
and to the new pot, to tap water and the tamped soil
of repeated generation, not knowing
what to make of this your
tenderness, God in these hands that do
not know how to say
otherwise—
blinding God, hear this prayer
amaryllis.

SKUNK CABBAGE

I let myself be drawn, I let raw bottomland
come take me into the *sanctus* and deep *sanctorum*
of the wild desire to be no other
                            than grapevine,
scantling sumac broken on the ground, beech leaf,
bracken, and this musk of decay and sulfur
borne aloft where I stand.

Even so, I've nearly crushed what I'm looking for.
Right by the side of my boot,
in the leaf mold and black muck of still wintry wetlands,
this first kindled uprush,
                     spring disguised
in shades of deep burgundy speckled with gold, swelling
turbans, sharp-tipped and silks ablaze—

such miracles, I have to throw a sop into the thicket
of the mind that isn't content to see
simply
       bruised, brawny blossoms.

Old Buddha's topknot (I whisper)—hallowed
onion dome in Kiev. The heart's own quiet Taj Mahal
resplendent in a niche of dawn.

Now I remember my compline vow—just to breathe
in the single wing of the wind
as it touches lightly the hollow of my throat.

No more gazing into the patchy mirror
of the swamp, no more
hoarding and hallowing, no more gaudy prayer.

Oh, what would it be like to be blessèd? to live
as the poor in heart must live,
                            inconspicuously
carried on the long wind of no beginning or end,
lifted into such presence I'd be faithful, I'd forget
to say anything back—

though it's likely, however unadorned
the moment, hushed
the canticle,
              sufficient the blessing,

I'd still have to hum, just a little.

POSTCARDS IN MARCH
to Henry

I
   from Portland, 1998

No shape, no size, no syllable—
no sign of you yet.

You are not even a speck of pollen,
not even a mist in the mind of the flurried willow.

Nor a snowflaked
facet in a blue dragonfly's wing.

Or you *are*, and are entirely equal.

What direction do I face
to speak to you,
who have no face?

II

Here is the old green pond before the frog jumps.
Here is the hollow nostril, bronze and stupendous, at Nara.

Be the japonica, whose flowers fall.

III
   from Pella, Iowa, 1999

In soaring dark and dawn fire equally at home,
you are born, back east

under the red-winged blackbird's
riding the rippled arc of a steep, stripling wind—

you who draw us back, before the alphabet of breath,
into the wild provenance of song.

IV

We're marooned in a heartland of winter corn stubble.

What's left of the original, inland ocean,
switch grass, side oats grama,

little blue stem, has been sown into a swatch of earth
and put on display.

Heartset on survival, they call it *prairie*.

At Red Rock we are taken to see the bald eagles
in the bare oaks by the river.

Over us their high, unfinished cries.

V
   from Cumberland Island, 2000

Morning's the whistle of a boat-tailed grackle.
A zigzag of pelicans slowly unzips the horizon, sun
spilling from a seam in the pocket of indigo and gray—

much as your father strikes a match
and you're all attention.

First the little curls of blue and yellow flaring up,
then the whole roar of the fire, a hissing
if the wood is wet, a spew of sparks out the flue—

but I wish I could see what you see.

Without words in the way, fire lifts its wings
inside you—
            as just now in me

a frothy flaunt of whitewashed cloud rushes east
across a clear vowel of sky,
boisterous angels edged with flame.

VI

In the forest of live oaks and palmetto a northern parula
lets fly its *pe-tse pe-tse pe-tse*.

An armadillo scuttles its snout through the leaf cover.
Holy idiot,
            it doesn't see me.
I'm rolling branch, Spanish moss, the fern called *resurrection*.

A sudden canopy of ibis, white with black-tipped wings.

VII

And who is Henry?
            Mothermilk and waterbath
            a tumble on the rug
            Cuckoo clockfire on the hearth
            a great big hug—

it's all one, and ripe, and rippling.

A line of pelicans, single file on a thermal—one flap,
two flaps, three—they glide together.

IONA CANTICLE

From Caolas Annraidh to Traigh Mhor, from Dun I to Port of the Coracle,
I praise your fanks and skerries, cnoc and loch, machair and port,

each carraig and cave, all the ground on which I have stumbled or strode,
  gully and meadow, hollow and moor.

I praise the four roads that, crossing, make this song of ascents.
I praise the wind that threshes the marram grass, and the rain.
I praise wheeling clouds, their dark muscle; they, too, are pilgrims.
I praise the fire along the length of my body, salt and sun at Sandeel's Bay,
  where I listened for voices, hearing only my own.

Strong praise for the stones, green serpentine, feldspar, pink gneiss, tumbled
  centuries of stone heaped for penance
into cairns at Port a'Churaich, and the roundy gray ones
humbled into the open cell at Port Beul Mor where I sat with my longing
  and my fear.

Quiet praise for the shieling below the Hill of the Quern,
where I kept silence, where silence kept me.

I praise rook and song thrush, gannet and grackle, skylark, and the one robin,
  ark of canticles,
which from its perch inside the Abbey's rubble walls sang in three voices,
  "I am God."

Gardens I praise, lush with globe thistle and rose, agapanthus, pink hydrangeas
  bright as fishing floats.
I praise the outcast, the stubborn, shallow-rooted, and lowly. Sea thrift,
  stonecrop, sea holly, bell heather, and ling. They make my heart glad.

On the machair one morning, I turned in a circle, as a child would, arms
  flung out, alone with the island, just by the Hill of the Angels,

unable to know the source of this joy, and yet
given it.

I praise the bog and black ditch, dark night, and the wind that took everything
    from me,
ragged, uneven gusts,
                    and the rain that peppered the window glass.

How wide the night is, how it refuses
to fear the untethered path it furrows into that fire and immensity we call storm.

How distant we are from that fire, and how near.

In the long wilderness of my wandering, I give thanks for the sudden gift
      of a soul friend, companion of the way, brother of my prayer,
anmchara and vicar of my heart,

who laughed with me, and wept, and sang.
I bless the voice that said my name wholeheartedly, the flesh that held me,
      and released me.

Now I understand I am not alone. All those I love journey with me
over the road of the dead, into Reilig Orain, through the door wide and narrow
      as a wound in the heart.

I praise the one body. All the hands that prepare the tables in kitchen and
    church nave, and the voices that bid us eat.
I praise broken bread, the fire of wine in the belly.

Down from the Hill of the Seat, down from the Hill of the Herdboys, down
    from the Cliff of the Streams,
I tramped moor and machair through the abbey of the flowing air.

Here I tilted with Orion into the orisons of the wind over the sea road
    of the saints.

Here I ran with the white horses of the sea.
Here, after compline, saw the brand of a star sear its way out of the deep,
   and back into it.

Here I rambled, fragments of rainbow, holy intervals of light, Hebridean, pouring
   into the sea that surrounds us always,

I mo chridhe, I mo ghraidh—

Iona of my heart.

HOUSE OF STONE AND SONG

I

To lie very still, held at the dark margin of the morning,
      dwelling nowhere—
who is not glad to be alone like this? More bare than

any prayer can pray me. Or to wake first, in just light
      as one by one the birds
raise their cadenzas and solos, chips of song

da capo, delicato, con fuoco—far off and near, random
      layers of song in my ear,
bringing withindoors stubble field and swamp oak,

mist in the hollows and wooded ridges. Spires of dark cedar.
      The shadblow, the yellow
blur of the willow by the shallows. Bringing withindoors

cantabile, acciaccatura, hermit brown, red-winged
      or hooded, green-throated
or blue, burnt sienna, rose-breasted or bronzed,

the pure wild sound of the world.

By the window the lilac, not yet full out, slants
      to a thicket of shadows
thrown on the bedroom wall. On a shadow branch

the tiny shadow of a bird, lilac the tremor of its throat,
      lilac the scent of its song,
and the roof of this house hovers over me like wings.

Now I know, without having to see it, how the pond fills
      with milk, with saffron,
with the whole sky's intimate incandescence.

II

Chip, chip, chip—now the sound of metal on stone,
    not a bird, it's Barry Patch,
stonemason, lover of stones and the uses of stone
    for the dead, for the living.

Goonies, potatoes, bones my husband calls the stuff
    of the walls he builds at the margins
we've cleared from the woods. He tells me
    not to steal the words,

so I give them back to him here as *field stone, blue stone,*
    the granite and gritrock
we'll walk on when Barry finishes his work—
    which now resembles, in the early

stages of labor, ruin—dug trenches and red string, rubble
    that's maybe useful, maybe not,
all the markings of a dig, as at Xochicalco. In the ruins
    one sees plainly

the power of the unfinished. The stones whisper, *Know*
    what we aspired to know, do what we dared
and couldn't, complete us, the fierce glyphs burning into
    sky, a smudge of bougainvillea.

Chip, chip, chip—Barry's squaring one stone to fit
    close on another, each one
finding its place in what we might call *patio, terrace,*
    moon-watching pavilion,

a room whose roof is air. Barry builds it on shelf rock,
    on sand and stone dust,
keeping us part of the broad ledge of cedars and laurel—
    anchoring us, much as the house

we love in Bear Run, Falling Water, is moored over
    impermanence and falling asunder.

And I think, moving now into a morning of tasks
    I can and cannot finish with,

how *soul* must be something unfinished, or never begun,
    or lapsed. Must be *no thing* at all,
at best *attentive*, a flowing attempt to form walls
    around a small glint of light,

that hint of abundance momentarily flashing, rarely
    up close, barely sensed—
if sensed at all, so likely misapprehended one keeps on
    inquiring—if only into the next room,

    where the secret is, hidden behind
stone walls, disclosed within undivided light and air.

III

Because we live in a country where no one I know
sings to God in the streets,
I'm given to wandering past margins of fern and wild honeysuckle,

following the burr of the tanager, that lazy, drowsy
dozy buzz of triple notes
tied close together. I'm tethered and led, *legato,*

deeper in, beyond cedar field and hardscrabble, through
grapevine, bullbrier,
globes of rhododendron and laurel lamp-lighting my way

over Indian graves and wetland, hellebore and hummock,
into the tall trees where
that flash of pure fire finds its high-branch summer niche.

Perhaps I want to be the crazy woman
who lives on roots and berries
in the only woods abandoned to her, perhaps a woman

inhabited, immersed, left open to the rain, a lit fleck
in the black eyes of the doe
who does not startle at the sight of me, a praise song

composed by the tail of a snake as it slithers into the rocks,
by the scattering of raw light
through the oak leaves—a generous rubble—

by the coyote's treble and the wild turkey's guttural call
taken in, this earthy music
dowsed for in the deep well of the woods, tasted,

taken into my body, alone and full, wind and stream.

IV

But yours, wise sojourner, is the art of recollection—
after home-leaving,
               home-coming,
bringing with you "something perfect for the kitchen,"
for the table a blue bowl, for the mantel a Tibetan
oil lamp cast as the body of a bird.

You rescued once a weathered piece of a push broom
from along a railroad track,
the bristles gone—
               but the pattern of absence
ground in there, and the patina of the seasoned wood . . .

It takes a quiet eye to see, a single heart to love.
*Blessed are the single ones . . . for you shall find
the Kingdom. You came from it,
you shall go there again.*

And so you put a road to nowhere through these woods
that were once abandoned fields
                       and built this house.

You dowsed for the well, and when we married
in the living room, after the few words we'd planned,
you took my face into your hands and looked

and looked, in your eyes such a shining it startled me.
To be so recognized.
                      To be found.

As when wind catches up the sun and billows it
across dark water—such a shining
that we are held and sent forth at once.

Something flashes out—who can say what it is?
In its wake,
           a net of light to catch our words,
and the words still holding us here.

V

When by accident he struck the stone, and it fell open,
as a book will,
           half by half,

Barry saw the stones were a pair of wings, matched
exactly, and he set them
                  soaring, in.

for David

ICON

Thou still unravished—but we would
cut the cedar clear through
bride and *brede*, and so with a chain saw's rude
disquiet we notched in a wedge and made to lay the tree
down where we wanted it,
watching a damson spew of dust
spun from the heartwood's slowly exposed,
unlikely burgundy.

How cleanly then the sixty years
of cedar cracked and fell
away—and gave us the wider view of the pond
we'd wanted. A heron hunched its neck and labored
from the reeds. And then there was quiet.
My job was to limb its long, antlered branches,
unruly evergreen, for kindling—too preoccupied to think
to bless it.

As is his custom, my husband
worked without swerving
from the task at hand, whistling, I swear it,
in full-throated ease. Listening, I was already serving
a distant master,
drawn into dream by the wedge of heartwood
we'd propped by the stone wall, its potent core
of muscadine a magnet.

That quiet well, that purple flare
set me summoning
birdsong buried deep in trees, all the unheard
stir and flutter inherent there in the early color
of sunrise
claret mornings before the rain comes on—
a blaze of song, a murmurous haunt of song, then
the ache of it. Pent there.

That's the thing of it, the pivot.
A wedge of wood, the quiet
eye's configuring, unacknowledged pain—
and I turned abruptly inward, having just glimpsed
an icon of you, John Keats,
a sketch Rublev might have made one sultry afternoon
in Rome as you lay wasted and spent
on your deathbed,

its pillow and shadow a chrismal nest
about your fevered head,
the diffuse gist of you gathered in what must be
sensed as presence—oh, but not unravished—
yours such a fervent, fraught
ambition I think of the young man I saw
before Orain's altar on Iona. He was already kneeling
when I happened in,

mute before the altar's wide board
and plain brass cross,
all his ardent plans unscrolled, placed boldly
there, given into the burden of the mystery
we hope to illumine.
He touched his forehead to the board,
still kneeling, and for all I know blushed crimson,
caught at such fervor.

I tried to ignore him. I looked
away into the cul-de-sac
and mudra my hands were making of emptiness.
Theophane the Recluse was right—most of us
are like shavings of wood
curled round the rudely opened core
we pretend not to notice, catching at musky
shadows instead.

But I couldn't ignore him—no,
we endured
each other's presence as one turns up a collar

against an intruding wind off the Sound and keeps on
                keeping on; we were kneeling
    but not impossibly. The wine of unease
and dissonance also a communion—
        or it could be.

        In the argent revelry and dark
              harmonies of your poems
    you seized at that truth, you bruised your way
into leafy passages, into the ordinary
            understory, searching
    what only can be known by touch and blunder,
or sensed in blurred discernings, in presage,
        solitude and wonder.

        In orchard joy, in the tease of sorrow
            you compelled
    response. Like you, but not yet betrayed
by the unimagined, the youth in Orain's chapel stood,
            scrolled up his papers
    from the altar's wood, straightened his watch cap
and—nodding off to the side, where I wasn't quite—
        he strode away.

        And then I stood where he'd stood
            full of blood and promise.
    And where you'd stood, coughing in the raw wind
perhaps, bareheaded, a pilgrim. Stood there in the ringing
            quiet without
    the comfort of word or gesture or vow,
sensing, within the silence, a harvest—for that
        is our labor, *touch wood*.

Complaint

*Pilgrimage refused? To be by psalm or angel bent—
refused? Standstill is part of it. And complaint.*

ICON

That man standing there, who is he?

Taller than the rest of us, statuesque,
as if on a plinth hidden
beneath the long white cloth
that fits his slenderness more like a sari
than a toga, he's bound his head
with a white cloth and whitened
himself entirely, the white of chalk
airbrushed across a blackboard.
His whole body masked. Nose
African, cheekbones Tibetan, mouth
a poet's—the one who refuses
to speak. Below him,
where the cloth flows like dawn
into the ground, there's a white bucket
for coins. Perhaps it's his smile,
wintered over, as after
great loss, that moves me to murmur,
much like one of Job's Comforters,

I had nothing to do with it.

In a lush confetti from the parade
of cherry trees sun-shadowy
on the city sidewalk, in full sun
men take off their jackets,
rolling up their sleeves, lovers bask
on the broad stone stairs that ascend
to the monumental doorway
of the art museum, whose hurly-burly
banners, red and yellow,
ripple over Saturday's tumble. Children
and tulips, the scent of cappuccino,

a red-and-white café umbrella . . . and now
the plink of a coin into that white bucket.

Taller than the rest of us, he tilts his head
and, in a slow mime, bows—
one lean arm moving outward, a sidereal
sweep over stones *white as mud*
from the stars, over the fields
of bruised camellias in the cloister of the gutter,
over petals and vomit and the homeless
voice I heard beneath an elm in Central Park,
Oh, the angel came down and peed in my pants,
but he wouldn't take me up. . . .

Sweeping out, sweeping over, his arm
a plume of new snow
over rock and rot, a single wing riding
the wind over the edge of the earth
becoming dark becoming light becoming dark—
and all the while the other arm
tucks in, toward belly and groin. He bends
low, he straightens, he stands radically still.
Again, the plink of a coin, so slight
a sound I could easily
not notice how it carries . . .

cries, songs, sounds of the dying,
it comes from everywhere

the whole nakedness, the whole humiliation

O one, O none, O no one, O you

IN THE HEART OF THE MOUNTAINS
Rereading Myrna's letters from 1987, Nicaragua

She writes: *In the heart of the mountains, between Jinotega and Puerto Cabezas, children fold themselves into their mothers' skirts when a stranger stares or comes too near. How can I tell you what this means? When the Contra come, you must dig into the earth and cover your child with leaves, you must lie there without food, without water, all day, all night, breathing so little your body looks dead. The Contra say to anyone who would deliver vaccine to the villages,* Te pasemos la cuenta, *we will kill you. Only Julio dared carry the serum in a thermos to Cano Sucio. To remember this man burned alive in his truck, I study a small red fence around emptiness.*

I finish reading what Myrna writes.
In the heart of the mountains, I finish reading
about the two nuns she found one morning
in the trash, in the weeds, their rosaries
and their measuring tapes wound around
their necks, their skirts torn open,
the sleeves of one habit torn off, stuffed
into this one's vagina, into that one's mouth.
Found them one morning, in a ditch
so near the village she could still smell bread
baking in a makeshift oven. The nuns had
come to teach sewing classes, reading classes—
(*How can I tell you what this means?*)

I concentrate on the oven, a huge black pot
with two "ears" (*How can I tell you?*)
(*vagina*) (*mouth*). Once the pot is lifted
from a pit in the earth, the bread's turned out,
torn into hunks, doled out. The pot has a cover,
flat and square, wide enough to support
a fire of dead branches. I concentrate
on the makeshift oven, on the bread,
carefully inverting the elements—fire on top,
the cover next, the pot, the pit in the earth.

I am learning how to make of easy sorrow
the bread of grief—not just
for the nuns, nor for Julio, nor for the children
with mountain leprosy, the scars on their legs
like tree bark. I put Myrna's letter facedown
in the sun. I remember the guns
we floated by parachute down to the Contra—
guns the Pentagon called "gauze bandages."
In the trash, in the weeds. I remember
years of protest and relinquished protest,
the fine print of every protected good intention.

This is Preston, Connecticut, and how quickly
the cries of the doves
fold themselves into the scalding crescendo
of spring sun—how quickly
the swamp maples (*fire on top*) obscure
that small red fence in the heart of the mountains.
How can I tell you what this means?
(You must dig into the earth and cover your child.)
(You must cover your child with leaves.)

LISTENING TO RAMÓN
Cantina El Peregrino, Isla Mujeres

In the throbbing cantina, within the lyric
swelter of the songs, I hear gunshots—
no, paper napkins drawn taut over the lips
of shot glasses, then the paper snapped,
a loud report, as one more lout
knocks back the ancient fire against
his throat and banks it. But my eyes
do not swerve from his. I hear only
the music he is singing with his *amigos*—
and beneath the music, in the voice
beneath his voice, what else?
Beneath the drums and the mandolin,
below the notes of the long flutes
whose names I've forgotten already,
behind the guitars, inside the small
sacks of seeds and shells that make the sound
rain makes on the leaves of the *almendros*
at night when I listen to the wind
and to the dog chained outside my hotel
howling, beneath the howling
I hear his name, *Ramón*.
Perhaps I give him a name,
perhaps I just know it, I don't know.
I look at him too quietly—but I would eat
this music if I could, he sees this is so,
I am not just the quiet *gringita*, no?
Or I am,
 for in truth I cannot
order a full breakfast in Spanish or talk
to the girl at the hotel desk
about even the wind, colder than I'd expected
on this island of palms and sun and American
hotel chains—though more than wind
has closed down the hotel that never opened

on Playa Cocos, where the winds of cold cash,
withdrawn suddenly, depressed
the thatched *palapa* the architects planned
for the grand arcade and hotel entrance,
where the waves dash their azure to a white
froth on the shell of it, stucco and tile.
And does it matter, one less hotel,
one less windy beach for some man to walk
with a sling of coconuts and a machete,
crying *Cocos, cocos!* What would it matter
to his son? I let myself imagine
Ramón has a son, much like
the boy I've watched learn to walk
in the *zócalo*, near the gazebo
that houses El Señor and the Kings in red tulle.
Grown, he will mend tangled nets
with the fishermen at dawn or sweep
the streets down with soapy water,
hours before the tourists stumble out.
He may peddle Hondas, golf carts, drugs.
Run a tour boat north to an island
that stinks of magnificent frigates
and gulls. Or fish lobsters, wipe tables,
play an endless game of hoops in the plaza—
but he will put an old jar of plastic blue
carnations at his mother's grave,
watching the sun ripen the cemetery wall
and bloody the wings of the angel
that holds one finger against her lips,
shushing the angers he might feel clearly.
He will be happy and not happy
within the stark lines of tile and walls of pink cement.
With a machete he will slice weeds
from the hotel gardens and watch without
comment the German or North American tourist
pay fifty dollars to swim with the dolphins
in a Yucatán lagoon, saying afterwards,
It made my whole vacation. And he will

follow the primitive god of the sun
to Cantina El Peregrino and sing
as his father sings, complaints
as seductive and soft as an open shirt—
> *Caminando, caminando*
> *Voy buscando libertad.*

And while he sings, in Chiapas, in Oaxaca,
los Indios, they are rising. What does it mean,
they are rising? I have not seen the bodies
that rebel and swell beside the road.
They are shadows in a war that begins
and may only end with workers paid
their wages in tortillas and salt, shadows
much too familiar or too strange—
stranger now as the music stops,
and the gringo boy at the table near me
licks salt from the back of his hand,
calling for more tequila. He disgusts me
and he interests me, with his girlfriend
in her too short floral shorts and floral halter,
this vacation the bargain they paid for,
cheaper than St. Tropez. And the singer?
He can live on the air he sucks
to sing these songs—*la paz, la justicia,*
what do they care? I watch Ramón
watching me watch them. I watch him
smile and see me look down at my hands—
supple and long, only moments ago
tapping the table with rapt attention.
I want to dance, I want to speak to him,
I don't know how. If I should
cross this room, going over to him,
standing close enough to smell
his skin, his wet hair, the cotton of his shirt,
I think he would fumble his cap, and say nothing,
> nothing to say.

Turning back to the hotel, walking slowly

back, I shake my head and give
an uneasy smile to the waiter on the patio
folding the napkins for tomorrow's tables
of fine linen and fruit, at his elbow
the latest ancient images of war
unearthly in the screen of televised light.
I promise to remember, I say to the fruit,
feeling as foolish as fervent. I promise
to remember the napkins and the empty
chairs, Ramón and the bodies
sprawled beside the roads—and by the stairs
that curve down from the veranda,
the toy musicians. Cast in terra cotta,
put down to play before a wall
grown lovely in blooms that purple the air
with extravagant scent, doll-sized, Mexican—
they hold silent instruments. They wear silent smiles.

ELEGY IN SOVIET GEORGIA
July 1985

When we tell how we sang together
the night of Bastille Day in Tblisi,
we tell it with a hitch
in the harmony, our voices braided
together in the manner of true
Georgian song, gusto and grief
in counterpoint—I remember
stone streets, pots of bright flowers
hung from balcony apartments,
apricots big as fists, bread baked
in beehive ovens, a woman
sweeping the street with her broom,
singing to herself with the thrift
of a steel blade stropped
to the scrawny bleat of a goat
beneath the minor-key majesty
of mountains.

           Before *glasnost*,
on the night of Bastille Day in Tblisi,
our uncle's friend Jhambakur said
he'd join us for dinner in the Intourist
hotel we knew no ordinary Georgian
could set foot in. His daughter had
baked three cakes large as wagon wheels,
hazelnut, strawberry, red currant.
He ordered champagne and chocolates
put on the tables. There was a piano,
a jar of flowers we'd harvested from
a ditch near a mountain vineyard,
tables of extraneous hotel guests—
cool East Germans, impassive Georgians,
the rest flamboyant Americans,
their flamboyant host and his daughter
Nestan, a shy concert pianist.

We sang "La Marseillaise." We sang
whatever indigenous songs we thought
we could remember—"Swing Low,
Sweet Chariot"—and then
Jhambakur arose, florid and tall,
and began the baritone of a Georgian song.
A whole table of lusty Georgians
joined the counterpoint, we cut cake,
the Germans sang something Bavarian,
Nestan roused the piano, we danced.
Jhambakur sang
                louder than anyone.
Joy welled from his body with the dignity
of grief. Around him, the party swirled.
Outside, stars. A black sky. Stone streets.

They wouldn't enter the hotel next morning.
Nestan and her father stood outside
the glass door with gifts, smiling—
wool hats of a type in the region,
a red rose Nestan pressed into my hands
without words—what do you say?
We gave them jeans they couldn't get
on the black market, embraced—
and watched them recede into the crowd
on Rustavelli.
                The rose was
wound with paper up the stem, to buffer
thorn, I thought, putting the rose, as we packed,
quickly into a glass of water on the sill.
The water bloomed with ink. Unwrapping,
I could barely read her uncareful words—
*opening here, to come to the States,
I want, for giving a concert, if it's . . .*
We packed. We'd do what we could,
we'd write—for now, on to Kiev, to Babi Yar,
to farms and museums, a czar's palace,
acres of winter silence beneath the closed
sweep of grassed graves inside Leningrad.

In time we would learn Nestan died on the stones
of Rustavelli, shot by soldiers in a protest.
She was taking a shortcut home, drawn by
the noise of the crowd, too curious.
Her father lived, but declined to speak.
We could not learn if he'd been ousted or made
dangerous in the tumult we call freedom.
Only now, when I tell how we sang together,
the night of Bastille Day in Tblisi, over and over
I come up against a rubble of detail
from which to build this story, like a wall
we could climb over, if we could.
And it's now, only now, that I remember
how I shivered as Jhambakur sang,
how I let the rhythm take me, back and forth,
like the woman we saw each morning
sweeping the stones, quietly sweeping
the stones. Back and forth, no end to it.

Displayed among the relics of his personal
life, the poem asks for purity of heart
and mind. Then a closing image—
the moon, and flowers white as the moon.
This was the prayer of young Stalin,
a student of monks beneath the Caucasus,
the mountains steeply green when we saw them
in summer. The poem hung on a white wall
inside the Stalin museum. Outside, we saw
an open coffin carried on the shoulders
of men whose shirts were open. We heard
a woman crying aloud as she followed them.
I wanted to weep with a woman we didn't know
how to speak to. My prayer back then,
as now, is Sufi—*May our hearts be
shattered open, and the Great Space dwell
therein*—only now I ask, Teach us
what it means by *shattered*, by *open*,
by *heart*, by *dwell*, *space*, *therein*.

ELEGY FOR A DANCER

She knocks softly,
easing the door shut, the eloquent
bruise along the swell of her cheek
"an athletic injury." Can what she says
be true? I let her lie, I let
us sit there, tangled
in the roots of a vivid lie.

She leafs through her notebook—
I hear the pages tick,
                     still revising
silently my lines about a young girl,
used as a pawn, who sold fruit
outside an officers' club in Saigon,
smiling prettily, until one officer
bent her backward, tore off her clothes
to show that she was wired to explode,
then slit her throat.

Now she shows me her poem,
written about a photograph
that shows in close detail
a woman's dead body,
the men around it busy with autopsy.
She uses a fine word, *firked,*
to say how they take out her guts.
She likens the angle of the woman's
head to her own in the photograph
made just moments after she was born,
her small wet head of dark hair
turned obliquely aside.
She says she wants to write
in the voice of that woman.

By the way she turns in her chair, I know
she wants me to know her, and would
rather I not—she's not a child now.
But I knew her mother,
how she stitched her daughter's underthings
by hand, put by jars of tomatoes,
dilled green beans, spiced peaches.
In charcoal she'd draw for her daughter
the weathered faces she'd known
as a child—Assiniboine—their children's
school, and her own, built on the fill
from piles of uranium tailings
so radioactive the clocks in school
ran funny.   Her pain
she painted as thick twists of rope.

 I look at her daughter across the desk.
As a child she had eyes of clear amber.
She could imagine, beyond the horizon
of hills gone to rust in the smoke of noon,
our earth borne along on the silken
train of a beautiful woman in a dream no one
has anymore.   Her eyes now are smoky topaz,
yellow quartz. She fingers her bruised cheek,
then says softly, as if she isn't saying it at all,
how she has one life openly at school—
at night she's an exotic dancer.

It's not what you think, she says,
but I think *sequins, smoke,*
roving men who tuck money
into her shiny halter, then go outside
with their women, in their heads
a savage tempo.   What I can ask, I ask—
my desk and the floor of the office

swept by the tangled shadows
of trees leafing out, leafing through
the window and the scent of beer
and embalming fluids. Then she
eases out the door—
she doesn't want any womanly advice.
She leaves me Vietnam; she has her bruises.
I have this poem, its record of pain at a distance
as a gust of wind thick with lilac crosses
my desk and its litter of books,
bringing with it her voice, without
its mask of nonchalance—
I am your dead daughter.

What I hear is heartfelt, never mind
that I alter the words at their source,
lifting them from a page of raw earth in a book
by chance left open to the wind—
not quite what the Vietnamese prisoner
uttered, so crazed by pain
he couldn't bear to say himself
straight out,
              desperate, and daring to sustain
beneath camouflage some small dignity
no one can snatch at or plunder.

PRIMARY REFLECTIONS: AFTER READING THE CHILDREN'S FIRST LETTERS TO GOD

How did you know you were God?
                              Charlene

In the yellow pail of salty river water
on the porch, inch by inch
the jimmy crab keeps on extracting
a softer replica of itself
from the intricate selfsame hard
shell and armored pincers,
each narrowly jointed hook and angle
of its self-devised defenses
sloughed. "It proves there's a God,"
says my grandfather. Oh, how I scoffed
at his simplicity! But he believed it.
The York River's blue and gold,
reflecting the sky's infinitude,
showed him God as Light, God
shedding form after form, nebulae
and jimmy crabs somehow
implied in a vulnerable self-revelation
downwardly extending itself—
the original *How do I know?*
still flickering in the syllables
of fireflies and stars, in the seamless
word of the turning world.
                    When I ask
Is it so? I remember the light that day,
white gold on the porch near the grass
and bank of trumpet vine and the pier
overlooking the tidal river's ebb and flow.
Intent on its hunger, a heron lifts into riverlight.
And it's heartbeat I hear, only heartbeat
rowing the air to the opposite shore. If only
I could surrender to that intelligence.

*Instead of letting everything die and having to make new ones,
why don't you just keep the ones you have?*
Jane

In late March the stiffened ruts of the lane
are gnarly as the limbs of the old maple
Hobart Mitchell loves and will not let
the power company cut to clear their lines.
Snow dusts the ruts, dusts the patches of ice.
Out of the swirling cold, the red-tail
billows down the center of the frozen lane,
keeping its distance from me, ten feet,
less—but still on the move, its compass hot
on the season ahead. The banded red
on its tail is the red of rust and old blood
and humid weather in the heart. Wide
hand spans of feather and muscle, mottled
with white, his wing shawl. And my God,
it's glorious how quietly into the quiet
this bird goes, soaring over the opening field
whose pond holds all shadows close, then
lets them go.

Dear God, how come all the things you say are in red?
Joanne

Color of blood as it brims, color of nectar
for hummingbirds, stop signs,
the garden blushed carmine with roses,
thick flesh of Snake River sockeye
before it's been seared on the grill—
red gets our attention. But suppose
the eternal Word in the text weren't
so separate. Suppose each red morning,
I unfolded the newspaper and found
all the words red—headlines,

scoreboard, weather: red.
White House, Garden Club, Pentagon:
red. Very red, a field of burning
Haitian heads. And the American general:
"We knew the problems, but we didn't know
the numbers." And the numbers red.
In red, I'd read how gravid salmon get
upriver by barge to bypass the dams
and hydroelectric falls, the Corps
of Engineers who herd them red—
red muscle, red milt. In red I'd remember
the human zygote, how it splits,
splits again, and cell by cell evolves
in a fetal sequence of vertebrate kin—
fish, amphibian, bird, small mammal,
small human mammal. Lord, here we are,
upright and not so humble
on the ocher earth we are part of,
each sunrise word of you incarnate,
incarnadine, endangered.
Ferret, cougar, curlew, wolf.
Sperm whale, swallowtail,
spindly Haitian, Asian, African child,
sea otter, leopard, each rain forest
and urban dwelling one of us
given in syllables as red as the paired
tanagers I watch for, each spring
returning to the patch of evanescence
and sheen we call scrub oak and wetland,
tucked now between the convenience mall
and the new casino, just off scenic Route 2.

COLLECT

Autumn wind scatters the petals of the cloud tree.

When I let the wind grow within me as well,
light
      shivers off the blue skin of the Sound,

a sharp-shinned hawk rides the billow

beyond the coastal
edge of tupelo, pepperidge, black gum—

three names for the one tree
soonest red
        in the salt marsh.

What thou lovest well is hidden
nakedly, not withheld.

Prayers are not enough. You must do something.

EPISTLE TO ROBINSON JEFFERS

Sick at heart, I want poor bitch Cassandra,
your hawk-faced girl, to mutter in my stead
truth to power. Close on the cusp of the new century,

Jeffers, the public cant appalls—but we will
test our warheads, eat poisoned meat, breed
armies of indolent self-congratulation,

and the greed . . . no wonder I pack off to the hills,
to hermitage, Appalachian and eastern,
a towering headland, stone that overlooks a valley

silence so milk blue it could be an inland ocean
roiled by wind. *At the monster's feet, there are left
the mountains,* you wrote, one season of kettling hawks

and blood in the leaf. In raw early spring I've seen
red-tails share a common branch, the larger female
only then less contentious. What follows that calm,

you knew, was appetite—airborne, fierce
and free, sheer as fire. Were it so with our kind,
we'd use no rootless words—our lives

would be our words. *I, the song, I walk here,*
the Modoc prayer, would be prelude to passion
and plenty. You'd have us embrace *and* relinquish—

no more scheming, hoarding *things,* no more
believing their occult power will protect us
from ourselves. Just yesterday, awkward and afraid,

I clambered down the rock face and came to rest
at the root of its towering bulk. Alone
beyond wanting, I looked up the rough

walls of that native stone, sure I could feel it,
the quiet thundering within the sheath of stone.
There was no shining forth and fearful symmetry,

no glory passing by that cleft of rock, no mystery
of God, that imagined rapture of patience and passion
younger I hungered to see.

Oh, but there were massive storm clouds, a great
wild shining, bridled—naked power
compressed to stone. I reached out and touched

the simple truth of stone, and my body trembled,
as if met by a lover, summoned
into pain and darkness by an intrepid joy.

The massive mysticism of stone, you wrote,
having looked at it directly, worked with it, built
house and tower with it, hauling each stone from

the Pacific shore up the cliff, each stone cradled,
cursed, too, perhaps—stone on stone piled toward
hawks overhead and the trade winds and the stars.

Pain can shine, you wrote. *Beautiful, intolerable
God,* you wrote, turning outward
into the whole splendor of things, wings and wave-worn

skerries, stars in the ocean of night, even
the treacheries of empire, and the greed, part of it.
There is in me, you wrote,

*older and harder than life, and more impartial,
the eye that watched before there was ocean—*
before stone, too.

Bite the lip, then. Mountain and sea, granite cliffs,
fire and the thunder of stone,
the kearing of wild hawks in the wind—

be faithful, you tell me, to these. Look on what is,
and be faithful. Tell no lies,
however splendid.

ARCHAEOLOGY

You who come here, if you come, cannot know how it tasted,
                this hook of dried root—
whether its flesh were ocher, gold, color of wild mustard in a field.
You'll have seen photographs of harvest, if archives last longer
                than houses.
You'll think, whoever lived here had a taste for the holy—here is
                a monk with no hands to fold in prayer,
none to protest the imperial episodes, their wars.
And this—was it a flower? Did the woman (was there a woman?)
                wear it in her hair,
this blue whorl of a tidal wave and night-blind wind?
You say it may have sprung out of a fetid wetland log—
and in the twisted root of dream, if you still dream, *parasite*
                turns to *paraclete*,
a word pebble as whole as the blue stone earring tumbled in with
                the midden of mussel shells and chips of china.
Who lived here? Ask the corn husk masks. They watched the man
                and woman, like a mist,
drift over the threshold of a door frame that stood, despite everything,
sentinel a while. They let the screen door fall gently to,
they knew where they were going, just down the road, past the bog
                and its stench of mutant frogs,
a rotted sump of skins and carcasses. They knew what it was to lose
                everything. They gave away
their bodies, as the monk his hands. When they prayed—if they prayed,
                and only for the bland
safety of the dead bolt, the comforts of ownership—it was not
                to the wild throb of fire
God is, but to its humbled image. Icon and evidence. These you can store.
There was the skull of a beast hung on the wall, and a tree grew out of
                it, once.

Confession

What nakedly wants, wants nothing. What can I want when want, the fact of it, creates and cancels out?

PRACTICE FOR A REQUIEM

When I try to imagine their deaths,
an old story they loved for its ending
echoes instead—
Whither thou goest, I will go . . .

and I set my feet
down roads, returning to a home
across whose threshold
I find bitter herbs,
different bread,
an earthen jar
in which to age the wine
of suffering.
                    Where have you been?
they ask like abandoned children.

Once, in the backyard,
they showed me
gently to close into my fist, then loose
into glass jars, the fireflies
that winked on and off
in the thickets of dogwood,
fig and plum—

so many little lights
I thought of stars
as I screwed the lid
on tight and punched
constellations of air holes in.

I held a bounded universe
between us,
and they and I, each one of us
by turns, held the jar up,

eye level, our faces
other and fitful in that light.

Now they look out the window
into the night. They want
me to tell them
stories, as a wanderer, come home,
would. *Look*, I say, and the moon
rises, august and harvest—

the moon, whose eye
is single,
its whole body full of light.

I have only this blind
feel for roots,
the depths
words take us to.
See with your own eyes—
autopsy. Threshold,
a relative of *wound, return*.

WHITE IRIS, OLD MEMORY
Dorset, England, ca. 1850

The last night of the illness, I walk out
the great house of gray stone, out into the rain,
making sure I get soaked, my nightdress
weighty with rain, opaque and cold. Thirsty
in the green blades of iris, diamond-pointed,
one with those ruined white blooms smudged
with blue at the throats, I stand as tall
as I can, listening to a stillness within me,
the source I'm returning to gradually,
without knowing why. At my wrists, cuffs
of lace fold like petals of the iris crushed
in wet rain. Behind me—suddenly, the light
of yellow windows imposed on the grass,
a walkway of light on the garden just reaching
my hem. Now they will find me, the husband
whose name I choose not to remember,
our child, the shrill family. And he comes,
murmuring my name, wraps a shawl
round my shoulders and guides me back in.
I'd rather he hit me. In the hall, held aside
by the woman who mothers him for me, the child
stares, his eyes the bore holes in the lid
of a barrel. And the rest, they recede,
shading their candles from the wind.
Upstairs, I watch his hands, let them
change me. Whose hands are they—whose?
Now I'm folded into bed, a length of fine
linen, the bed curtains drawn on two sides.
The candle, placed well out of reach,
makes the dark only deeper. He sits by the bed,
this man who has said to me softly, firmly,
"The part of us that knows God is God,"
receding into the study's dark secrets, his books
and charts. Now he sits by the bed, he studies

my face, growing pale as I grow flushed.
Something opens inside me, a feeling of light—
but again he distracts me, claims me, frets.
I push farther back in the pillows—
then I'm up by the ceiling, looking down on myself
in the bed, on the candle, on his taking my wrist,
calling out of the room for our son. He's afraid
of this dying. I would comfort him, but cannot.
The room brightens. How lovely, I think,
my body in its linen, how lovely and wasteful.
For what did it teach me? A woman lost in music
never mastered, in opinions never owned, in powers
never felt. Now the light swells and swells.
The candle fills the room with its presence.
And I remember. One moment—standing in wet
wild iris by a brook, hearing from open windows,
the windows of this stone house, such music—
and before I could swear I would marry it, felt
a single imperative, one effortless clarity . . .
then turned back to myself. A chit in a torn dress,
the barrel maker's daughter—empty, ambitious, low.

THE FUNERAL

Although there were some who strew the grave
with their bitten nails, expecting
them to sprout up lilac trees,
the great-grandnephews
were in the pantry telling
jokes about anatomy.

Starlings peered from the telephone wires
and the shadows of branches blew over
all the assembled, each
in his way sinister as the orange
dress of the alcoholic aunt
who found with a razor
her cross purpose
on her wrist and was pulled from the bath
in most everyone's opinion too soon.

All the great-grandchildren were found
to look like the grand original. Fat
runs in the family.
I prayed for continence.
In the next field the horses grazed,
their great pikes hanging down.

DEEP WATER

Love? The easiest
abyss, winding
dark water
at the base of sheer
overhangs
rock slides and a
going down fast
in water that does not
shrink from any
danger any plunge
depth on depth
until the whole ravine
fills, a branching
spring in which
I drink down
the full moon
and the crescent
winds stars suns
all gold and flame—
no cup no ladle no rim.

Once I was
taught the art of
place mats, chairs
a ram's head bowl
on the dining room table
filled with zinnias
and phlox. You want
I should do that
now? Good mother,
you must be kidding.

MANGO

> Three things are too wonderful for me,
>   four I do not understand:
> the way of an eagle in the sky,
>   the way of a serpent on a rock,
> the way of a ship on the high seas,
>   and the way of a man with a maiden.
>   —Proverbs 20:18–19

I

The day hot, the air wet felt,
each thought a runnel of sweat,
I take this champagne mango,
entering the monastery
of its plump flesh peel by peel,
crescent by crescent sliding
lush gold into my mouth,
savoring each warm shiver
of mango so utterly
the juice drips down my chin,
between my breasts, essence
of mango my barest wish.

Surely now
    the Beloved
will enter the humid void that I am,
and in a long cascade of desire
lick me clean.

II

Consider the sharp blade of the seed
within the bound solidity of silk—
how can we trust
such succulence, so mortal?
And yet I'd kneel at your feet,
each bare toe a tiny mango

to suckle. I'd tongue each one by one,
climbing slowly the trellis of entwined
clematis fragrant about your thighs,
just to the cusp of the orchid that roosts
in the aura of the body's ripe perfume,
nibbling my way there, nuzzling. . . .

III

I am offering myself to you. This is practice
for the shift in the mind that makes real
what can be glimpsed of God.
Far from the acute thrust and mutual solace
of such meeting,
                I say *mango*
as if it were prayer and orchard,
sheltering the fruit of my longing in a bowl
whose crystal facets refract and reflect
the white light that floods this table—
laying the mango aside,
                      until you are here with me
to enter its tawny vow of incandescence.

IV

It may be that words come together
but we do not.
          There is a pain, so utter . . .

it neither floats off, nor falls away,
is not embraced, denied, transcended—
unless in the equipoise of light

some call *sobriety*, others *grace*.

Add mango to the list of all that is
too wonderful for me.

I put my hand on my mouth and bow down.

ICON

Let whoever is sinless . . .
the man charged calmly, then
squatted back down,
making himself low,
lower than the elders, than me.
He studied bare ground,
the holy dust of the temple,
marking it with a swirl of his hand,
never meeting my eyes,
never looking at my body.
Or would they remain,
and stone by stone give me
the death I'd longed for?
A fire of thorns in the flesh
they were, bees blazing,
the fine hems of their robes
jangling with bells
and dried pomegranates, fresh
from the festal procession
when they plucked my lover from me.
Waving myrtle and willow tied
with palm, they came
to the bier my bedchamber.
Holding the citron, sign of harvest,
with the stain of psalms
on their tongues, they came to the bed
of the olive merchant's wife,
standing only long enough
to slake their need to shame me.
I had tipped my nipples with henna—
these changed from buds of the pomegranate
to ash, the wheat field my belly
to the shallow pit they fling the harlot in,
my hair to hyssop, the only sound

in my throat the rasped echo of their voices—
ráca, the cry of the raven
on carrion, unclean. *Oh, catch us*
the little foxes that spoil the vineyards,
catch us the foxes. . . .

Long before they caught me,
long before, a girl green and lyric,
I was marked for grief,
born with its shadow
beneath my eyes, beneath my feet.
In the time of tall barley,
in the time of almond trees
white with scent, little foxes burrow
into the roots of the fig trees,
to Sheol they follow the long roots
down to the dead we have spiced
and buried. How long I watched
when they put my Beloved
beneath the olive tree, when they laid him
naked into the orchard, how long
I prayed God put back the flesh,
God soothe it with balm and fine linen,
God give him back to my bed.
But he would not raise
the poor from the dust, nor from ashes
lift the needy, nor turn rock
to a pool of water, nor flint
to a steadfast stream. Instead,
my father gave me, like an ewer of oil,
to my Beloved's brother's bed.

Tell me, you who pasture in the lilies,
radiant and ruddy with your lawful
husbands, do you *think* when you
kiss his body, do you *think*
of the dead? When his hand
wanders the slopes of the garden,

into the nut orchard, when his tongue
finds the pip of the pomegranate,
and sucks, do you hate your pleasure,
do you stand aside from the bowl
of mixed wine and *think* yourself
ash, a razed field of arum
and cyclamen? Do you *think* yourself
husk, a pod of carob thrown
as fodder for cattle?
When his body moves fully onto yours,
and you're helpless as naphtha
brought near the fire—when, against
your will, fire rages
in the orchard that is your very own,
do you *think* yourself
a saddle quern grinding the corn
in early morning? Are you crushed
as olives pressed in Gethsemane,
are you spent with the grief of it,
the effort? Are you ravens
in a plague over Jordan? Are you
the grove the harvester enters,
beating olives down
with a long, gnarled stick?
In the cool of the day have you
slipped out of your body
and become its long shadow, calling
Drink deeply, O my lovers, drink?

Then how can you condemn me?
Ready to be sought by him who could not
ask for me, ready to be found by him
who could not find me,
I searched my heart and found
no sign of the faithfulness I wanted.
I was *rôsh* with its poisonous root.
I took my lovers as you'd take
a purge, my body

the lush flare of flesh that ripens
the vowels of pleasure
so like pain, my body
the toothy consonants, the knock
of bone on bone, the obstacles to union
that tell how like unfaithfulness
separation is. Once at midday,
my lover gone, washing the maquir
and sagebrush steppes of my body,
I scooped up the water and found,
there in my hands, a moon.
I put my face near, and I wept.
The royal moon by day,
the *Shekinah* of the waters—
this was not for one like me. And yet
there the moon was,
floating now in the common basin,
shining even as I carried it
out to the balm gardens, shattering
to a thousand perfect lights
as I poured it on the roots of the spikenard.
It was God-manifest, God-kindled-in-water
I gave to the purple spikenard,
and each burning stick
was *shûshan*, blossom of the rose—
for the fruit of love is fire.
Oh, but I was tinder that would not catch.
The fire met in me no fire. Touch me,
I was cold, I was resin
from the rockrose crushed, I was myrrh.

What you don't know from the story
handed down, he saw at a glance,
that man in the dusty robe
who knelt down, waiting,
as I was waiting. I stood still,
the elders shuffled their feet,
the hem of the priest's robe

a sistrum, a rattle in the throat
of one dying. Them I heard,
him I watched. How intently
he considered the dust, then wrote on it—
not so much a writing on, he drew,
not so much a drawing
as a drawing forth. I think now
I saw curling tendrils of fire
at his fingertips, or little whirlwinds,
now a swirl, now a circle, a spiral
within a circle, now the path of the moon
or the swoop of an eagle to its aerie
returning—it didn't matter
what he drew forth from the dust.
What mattered was the man.
He neither touched me, nor spoke,
nor looked at me. I stood
within my body, no longer yoked
to shadows, the shadows
burning. And then it was quiet.
"Woman, where are they?
Has no one condemned you?"
No one had—and from that moment
I was *no one*, too. "*No one*, sir," I said.

He was standing with me, so close
I could see the thorn of a thistle
caught in the cloth he wore, sweat
in the grooves of his nostrils.
Who is that, come up from the wilderness?
And still I don't know, I can't say.
"Go and sin no more," he said.
And I followed him
out of the temple courtyard, along
the lane of festive booths,
through the market's spices and oil
and wheat, the road bright as water.
He paused at my husband's door.

Moments after, I stood
where he'd stood, watching as he walked
out of the city, toward the mountain of olives.
I watched him go and stay with me.
I watched myself stay with him and go
into the house, sorrowing and rejoicing.
I was no more than he, and no less.
My husband, Clopas, took another
wife to bed—yet he kept me on,
he was good. I tend the garden. I sew
purple bands to the sleeves of his robe.
Now I bear witness to myself.
Before Abraham was, here I am,
brought back—a song in the night
when the holy feast is kept, a flute
when one sets out to the mountain.
The water I draw from the well
is good to drink. Blessed
am I among women. Over my door
are all choice fruits, new as well as old.

COLLECT

Just now in the living room of rafters and secluded summer light a wren
                is hurling itself, body and breath,

against the stubborn, self-watchful, hard transparency we call window,
                and it can't break through, nor avoid

its own desire, nor land there on the branch of shagbark just out of reach,
                nor be flung into the accustomed avenue

between the oaks, nor dip to the distant blur of brown mirage the pond is,
                never mind that I have opened

fully two doors and all the windows and stripped them of their screens.
                It doesn't realize its freedom.

I am its harrier, encouraging—if it's courage—with whispered cries:
                Go *on,* go *on,* go . . .

as it nears, then veers from its own release, retreating to a high rafter, huddled
                now into the pitiless solitude

that hasn't name nor motive, cause nor certitude nor solace. Who can praise
                enough—if it's praise—this last,

if it's last, sufficient and humble refusal? As surprising as the gathered
                urgency that lifts it, and soundlessly

takes it beyond *inside* or *outside, free* or *not free,* unevenly straight through
                the door of whirling depth and wind

                the wren in its lonely and passionate passage just now is.

for Joseph

EPISTLE TO THE FIELD IN ELDRED, PENNSYLVANIA

I must tell you now what I didn't need to say before, our flesh so close
we met in the blackberry blood on my tongue,
in the burning brand of sun on my back, in the shadows of high roiling
        clouds nomadic,

your body and mine wild lace and silver rod, heal-all and everlasting,
the sweet, mournful train whistle far down the valley
a love cry lifting from us.
                Then morning, tunnels of mist
in the hollows and over the coils of the river, red sun rising
orchid and mango, a gradual gold,

the whole body of the field riding that arc of awakening light, at the crest
the echoing cry of the harrier above low nests and thickets
and over the margins of the hills,
                until there was blue haze,
a dusk of deer, the vesper chorus of crows in the locust,
a last chirring of crickets—simply nothing more to ask for,

but there, beyond the orchard of wild apples, in a covert of beech wood
a wood thrush, rising and falling, watery and night-silver song,
as if to confirm that *prayer* and *praise*
                    spring from the same root
and river of milk. Your wild provenance

goes deeper. No words can touch it. I could spread my length to yours,
immersed in your coverlet of deer tongue and rue, whispering—
years of this—and come no nearer your mystery.

Yesterday I stumbled on bones, a leathery claw, a shawl of softly splayed
gray and brown speckled feathers.
                  Steady and clear
I felt no pain, made no promises. I have been prodigal enough with promise
        and vow.
No, this was different—I simply took it in.

I have eaten your apples, red-fleshed and sweet, or green and hawk-eyed,
        so sour I squint,
harvested wild flowers and berries, the summer-ripe moon,
roaming hill pastures rife with hawthorn, bracken fern, and bramble
or lush with aster and meadowsweet.
                            I've washed after love
in water drawn down from a spring deeply burrowed in your side,
drunk from the dipper hung north on a night hook of sky.

As close as breath, as close as death, you are in me, as the fossil prints of shells
lie snug in the shale of your rib cage and ridges.
Let them open my body when I'm dead,
                        they'll find in me
rust and gold, mint-ridge and river-bottom greens, a scent of rain
sweeter than perfume or musk. They'll find bindweed and mist,
a spaciousness I have called your presence, as your silence is voice.

They'll find hill and field, fruit trees flooded with the surf of starred blooms,
autumn's mourning cloaks and monarchs, and maples so gold
they seem a tumult of goldfinch anchored, then off in a flash of light, flying,
        flown.

Etched more deeply than any mark of father and mother, in me they will find you
and know
        that all my days you followed me, that all the long nights I was faithful.

To you I came like the wild hart thirsting.
Let us go forth into the field, it is written. *There I will give you my love.*

Compline

*Stalled or set out, on the midnight road I wait
for grace. The* not *inside the guise of what I want.*

COMPLINE

                In the time of night prayer, unable to pray
I open the windows to shadows that all day
                        went in a dial around solid oak
      and dried stalks in the field. *I lay me down*,
            drawn down to their sources.
The curtains shift, the moon crosses the web of the screen,
                    the wind carries hints of resin and salt
        from the alcoves of the pines, the Sound now the moon's
              ebb and flow in the pine boughs. I luff the sheets,
a billow of taut white settles down on my sex,
                    smooth along the cleft of my legs. My ribs
        angle like roots, and the breasts, small rabbits,
              wrinkle their noses, alert and still.
My soul to keep, I follow the hum in my ear, a single
                    G-minor note in the valley whose silence is
      shadow and still waters. *I lay me down*
            beyond dying, beyond waking and its many words
for *thou shalt* or *thou shalt not*, now only the widening shawl of wings
                  that lifts in the pine grove—*no one,*
    no one, no one—prayerful and mute.

PILGRIMAGE

Why do I take the back way,
along the sheep trod,
through salt wind and last
light, resisting
the tower and the standing cross
thrust darkly against
the azure evening sky
as it deepens and deepens
into illumined ink,
the well into which the monks
dipped their quills—
finding my way
by wandering the rim of far hills,
trusting the wind in my face
and the brief path
body makes into the wind,
moving ahead, or away from,
or toward, and never
arriving, unable to rest,
as if rest would deliver me from
mute inquiry
and the mission of solitude.
There the abbey is—a beckoning
quiet, a light
I keep circling and circling,
grasped by what I cannot grasp,
drawn inside
only by staying out,
rapt and roaming, at the margins
listening to the sea's dark breath,
how it ruptures
and heals, eddies
and is, the road behind me
dissolving in the dark.

STRANGE ALTARS

Who sends the mind to wander far? Who first drives life to start on its journey? Who impels us to utter these words? Who is the Spirit behind the eye and the ear?

To steady my heart I say these words, to keep me
      each morning
before the altar in my study, a footstool

      on which I have placed
the head of the Buddha, the gilt rubbed off,
      one lowered eyelid worn gold.

Fixed to a spike, the head of the Buddha's
      fit to a small wood block
for balance, not for permanence—the body of the Buddha

      gone its own way, the head
changed from temple plunder to exotic fragment,
      a bit of inscrutable ruin.

The topknot of flame, the *Ushnīsha*, geysers up
      like a gothic spire
from the skullcap of close corkscrew curls.

      Ears pendulous, nostrils
flared, eyebrows the wings of a seabird
      afloat on a thermal. And the mouth,

I love the mouth, how it's puckered in the loose
      serenity of a smile that lingers
when one's been kissed, the lover no longer

there in the room.
And so I sit, *certain of nothing*—some mornings
      not even that.

Who sends the mind to wander far—who brings it
      home? You think
this asking is easy? A rationed calm? An abeyance,

      flowing and cool?
Eat the question, you swallow fire—a ruthless,
      unoathed fire that

swallows you completely. Exactly what I want,
      the head of the Buddha
rests on the white rebozo I bought in Oaxaca—

      rests on a remembered
aroma of sweat and dust and dried herbs in a basket,
      ropes of *chile de arbol*

red as the shriek of the small pig hoisted behind
      a bright blind
of zinnias and callas, its throat about to be cut.

AT DÚN DÚCHATHAIR

From *dubh cathair*, black fort. On Inishmore, largest of the Aran Islands, at the brink of sheer or overhanging cliffs a hundred feet high over the sea, there is a single wall of immense thickness built of rough, unmortared limestone blocks. At either end, some of the length of the wall has been lost with the collapse of the cliffs. A gateway has also fallen into the sea. What remains is a slouching mass, dark against the southern sea spaces.

I

Wind-racked, high over the undulant clefts
of the shattered Atlantic,
                    if I turn away

from kind words meant as a caution and stand
at the edge of the cliff face,

it's just that the blue vein of the horizon
gets under my skin—
                    that just here,

blown on a shaft of wind, a rock dove
changes to a flinty dazzle

plumbing the distance fathoms down
barr aille into the unadorned air

and ruined syllabics
of Aran's wave-cut terraces, over *creachoileán*

and ocean,
            one sheer hurtle.

II

He's dead now, *Is mór an trua*. This the refrain
of Aran's *seanchaí*,
                what's left of them,

the poets, the old custodians of Aran's lore,
the strophes of their stories

embedded in the names for crag and sea stack,
storm beach, ledge—
                Aran
the book I try to read with my feet,
tramping overland from Cill Rónáin

along the worn boreen, up fissured limestone
recumbent in the field, over bald cenotaphs

a glacier polished—
                stone fallen, stone risen,
stone rising every which way, the walls

a clumsy lacework I look through to the sky.

With a field guide I can name what edges
things—thrift, lady's bedstraw, bugle,

bloody cranesbill. But when I ask the stones
to say their names,
              their syllables
blur in a thicket of consonants. *Carraig an* _____,

The Rock of . . . what is it?

        Rock of the Little Pig.
        Rock of the Corpse.
        Rock of the White Woman Drowning.
        Rock of the Hollowing Weather.

III

Hardly anyone left
who remembers the men who let themselves down
the headlands on ropes, nine fathoms down—

it's an art. All night on a ledge
the cliffman Mícheál Ó Maolláin of Baile na Creige

took guillemot and rock dove, wringing their necks,
thirty score in a cloth bag flopping—

also razorbill and cormorant. He needed
their flesh and their eggs, the feathers

for pillow and mattress, the fat for a smoky oil.
Oh ay,
        hauled up the cliff face next morning,
stooped with cold, hunched over his kill,

hauled up from An Poll Dubh, the black hole

of wild weather—
                      unless the clumsy fellow fell.
Is mór an trua.

IV

Evening comes to the damp grass, rising out of the stones,
the sea a smear of ocher.
                          Such is the power
of the unfinished, I stay long after

our companions, all but one, ramble back to Cill Rónáin.

Not enough alone, he uses his need for a cigarette
as excuse
            to wander off a distance,

discreet behind an open-worked stone wall, standing there
looking off to the sea—
                              one more lean and angular

silhouette of stone in the tumbled wall,
part of the meander

darkly set against a sky that deepens from green
to glassy cobalt into black,
                                until I can only find

and lose him by that pulsing ember, just one more
speck in the starry pageantry—

gone too swiftly into it.

V

Earlier than any *ailleadóir*, earlier than any cashel
or farm on Aran, long before it was
Árainn,

men and women lived among the stones and watched
their particular pole star

shift, and seem to fall, and seem to drown
in the well of the sea, pitched below the horizon's edge—

one sheer hurtle.

That's why they came here, whoever it was
built this tumbled nest of stone.

Not for ceremony, nor for defense, but to stand
at the mortal edge just like this,
                              hearing only
the panic wrung from the heart's

steep poise.

VI

                    Perhaps I am here after all
not to stand out, nor to accomplish.

Perhaps it's enough to wait among the stones, to stand
in the watershed of night wind
                              as the stars slide down

the steep, unfinished sky—

a small hinge
              of earth and emptiness—

and in the wordless song of flung spume and wind
taste that sweet word *death*

like a stone, sharp set, beneath my tongue.

COMPLINE

If, as we say, it's true
death's our common ground—
whose blood is it sucks upward in the mud
making the small
kissing sounds beneath my shoes
in the winter thaws? And at night why
am I still walking
beneath the banded clouds
that make the slender fields look light enough
to hover in the air . . .
never far off the harrier riding the
thermals, in that sharp eye no mist to curtain
the river's polished curve,
the slightest fever stirring in the tufts
its target, say, the winged-seed white of a throat,
a woman waking in panic
from years of solitude and dread
as the hawk haunts her bed, her field of blood,
our common ground—
if, as we say. . . .

REQUIEM: A POEM IN FIVE VOICES

*to the memory of the young men capsized and drowned
off the west coast of Scotland between midnight
and morning, December 13, 1998*

I

He'd have stood there, at the mooring place, in a reverie of stone and sea to read
    the running of the waves.
He'd have looked over to this island, darker than the sky, no lights below the
    mountain, none on the slouching coast,
none on the machair, strath, or hirst. None in the village—all smoored there.
He'd have whispered, *Fiddle be in my blood one hour more*—just two hours'
    sleep to trawling.

He'd have stood there a long time before the running waves, which are the
    houses of the dead. He'd not have said
beneath his breath, as they shoved off the shingle into the moon-ruddled sea,
    what his mother muttered in all weathers
when I set out, and our son kicked the waves within the sea of her body:

> *Protect me, O Lord, for my boat is so small.*
> *Protect me, O Lord, for my boat is so small.*
> *My boat is so small and your sea is so wide.*
> *Protect us, O Lord.*

Once in a terrible turnabout of storm, waiting for light at the hint of Torr Mor,
    he said to his mother, not to me—
I can, in the wuthering, feel how the sky reaches down, reaches in, and opens
    the heart, so quiet it is between the heaves.

II

I can hardly bear to look at it, the sea,
    at first light roiled and wind-scathed as I go
        out with the mothers to search for their dead sons.

                I look away to the sky instead, a sullen
          weaving of cloud, abraded and furrowed
into bands ash blue and black, a fine etched line between

as if incised by a burin. I could weave
          such sky on my loom at Tigh na Bearg,
                    but in pewter and silver with a shimmer of coppery sun.

          Set within the light, with driftwood and stone
     and a fishing net, it would make a fine altar to stand before
strong in our grieving.

At noon, above the shelly ground of Row You Can't Row Skerry,
          the sky's white, as harled and snowcemmed
                    as a cothouse. Over shingle and strand, over coast

               rough-skinned and speckled, finally
          into the raw suds of the tide, into gully and cave
I am able to look for them—

Oh, but how can we find them? The current out there's strong
          as a binding rite, swift in the hettle.
                    They write their names in water now, absorbed

               by a listening so deep it will be in dream
          if we find them, in dream if we find them now,
held fast in the port-a-beul of the sea.

In solitude I go inland,
          stravaiging over machair and moor
                    toward the lochan of the lapwings meadow,

               away from the sea, away from it—but always
          before me each footstep, sure I can see
small and formal a whorl ash blue as a blossom,

a limning of eddy and whirlpool, the sea
          as a curling of turf smoke, the sea as the wing of a rock dove,
               the sea as a holy well—

       this is the dreaming come on me,
   walking, awake in the whispering of my heart.
O God, give back the lost from the hoarfrost sea.

Let our dead come home to us, lift them
     from the dark place into limitless blue, make the sea
         willing, smooth as the silver of a spoon.

      Let our dead come home.
   Give them into the arms of their mothers
dressed in clove oil and geranium, nativity, and threshold.

Grant them psalm and oran. Give us rest.

III

We've never asked for much, so many troubles you could never find your feet.
I've seen my son, mocking
his father, cry out in the old way, "That's enough, or it winna go roon!"—
then laugh and put his glass down
hard on the table at Grant's. They weren't mortal drunk, I know that.
He wanted to live, to live here.
He wanted a wife to island with—without, it's fiddles and ale when the hills go
dun and cinnamon, and the sea
round the skerries swells to the luster of the sea that beat within him.
He wanted to live here.

Now I want the old angers
I felt when we went back, exiles on the excavated strath, and saw the low
stone outlines of cothouses
kailyards, stockyards, a corn-drying kiln, the skeletal clachan of my family's
family on Mull, a stone wall
their backbone, the spinal cord, our old way of life, pithed out.
Blessed be his glorious name forever—I have that choice,
and in the gowl of the wind, if I've the wit,
I've the fantasy retort, that cry of comeuppance when the tyrant's
taken lazy bed and cow,
poured out the milk on the hearthstone, quenched turf, set fire

to the thatch and turned round
to mock our raw grief. I say *our.* That's what we have for memory,
for history handed on, *that* and as much meal
as you'd blow off the top of a spoon.

Waiting for more rain, I'm composing, in the way of our great-grandfathers,
a pipe tune to echo
the wailed notes of psalms. Look off to the west—you can still see them,
the slave ships, refitted for emigrants,
set off for America, in the holds of their hulls a handful of earth.
I've less than that for a son now.

IV

Would you listen for me when the wind sinks?
Listen at the turn,
just at the peak of its flinging out fury
so far you'd swear
it could snuff the star flares.
Listen to the seethe
that moils beneath the currents of the Sound,
to the smoking surge
that scours the Bay at the Back of the Ocean—
there I claim my ben,
in the innermost, my heartbeat the muscular
hoise of the sea, my heartbeat the muscular stammer of earth waves—
mudstone and marble,
quarry, headland, spindrift, starwrack and strand
all tidal in the thunderous
stour of a torrent that has nothing to do with
what once I wanted, once I was.

V

When the sea madness comes on you, you go
stumbling through weedy boulders,

calling loudly to the sea,
                you strip yourself bare,
barren and self-forgetful you stride
into the tide of snow wreaths, into the sea,

smiting the tide swell, scooping and lifting
the running handfuls of the running waves.
You sing songs to the sea,
                pitch stone and shell and bracken
at it, cursing—then you pray,
lifting the brine to your mouth, mocked

and baffled, stung blind.
To love the wind and the salt wave and forever
be mocked, it's a bitter thing.

And so I promised his father, "When our son
washes up on the strand, I'll go
down to his body."
                And go as sure as the slopes
drop down to the sea polished opal and glossy,
the sunken sun a fire

dyeing the cloud bars and trade winds purple,
lovely the wild plum
bloom of the Mull mountains.
                Each day after
was like drinking from a glass already broken,
each night of storm

a pitching past the dinnle of stars, nearing that chasm
where the winds sink and a precipitous
murmuring,
           one continuous
unrolling of sea wave, tears through
what's left of your grieving, and you're nothing now,

displenished and lone, keen—an emptiness
one might live in, splendid and desolate

as a rock of light, if only,
                            if only one could stop
chiding the Lord of Storms, "For all you care,
we are dead," and *be*

the simple patience of breathing. A breath.
At times, I could be. And when he was there,
one white morning
                        there on the shore,
swollen and glotten, the glet still on him,
I saw he'd been eaten at.

Oh ay, when the sea madness comes on you, you go
into the grace of it, living as one
already dead,
               dying as one
who has lived into the sea's deliverance, its wild skewl
and dirl. And knows its nearness,

and whispers to it, *Come home, come home.*
I was just there with him.
I was just there
                      and nowhere. Clear-eyed.
Alone with it. How the world hurts.
Wind and stone. Seafire and shadow. A rain of stars.

COLLECT

In strict abundance
snow
ticks on the glass.
House
window
and black branch
gather, then
shear away
in a sudden outcry,
a call note
so bare, I sense
what scythes
between
each precise
flake
and gradual
petal—
so liminal, I enter
the sealed
petition
of the snow—
which has
neither
enviable rigor
nor curve of thought,
no stunned
solo, no
stubbornly
burnished
wing.

EPISTLE FOR JANUARY 19, 1999
to David Purdy

On the anniversary of your birth,
earth's iron season,
when the huddle and gnarl of brook water
running over stones stops, and the dark
New England trees are ribbed with snow,
and when, there on the North York moors,
where you are, the wind whelms and whelms,
I remember the New Year's full moon,
how it welled wholeheartedly
in the early evening and ripened gold
above the frozen pond,
and so numinous
it might have been a threshing floor, or the halo
of some Celtic saint, its beneficence
abundant as a harvest altar by the sea.

By now, of course, that moon has rolled away,
passing over your shoulder, drawn
back into radical, unbroken dark,
yet one more completed existence
spiced with a trace of what all parting
is—all the while, each one of us
too busy, too dutiful
to notice, too ready with complaint,
and yet at intervals translating ourselves
fully into gesture and act,
tending, rending, working the earth of the heart
as we must. For nothing grows to fullness
from psalm and possibility and prayer
unless ground is broken, worked
in runrig, turned and turned.

Tonight your birthday moon is new—that is,
a darkness within darkness, richly given.

May you close your eyes and breathe its musk
and miracle—may you savor and sense it
whisper by whisper on your pulse.
Just as, at Port a'Churaich, you flung
that black stone from you, entrusting
all sorrow and past joy go with it
into the tidal refuge of the sea,
so turn now and embrace
the earth-dark moon, its living mystery,
the light it bears and brings
down from the well of its various seas—
for you are here among us, and we are glad.

TENEBRAE

I

What is darkness, that I must enter it?
        What is night, that I must watch and wait?
Look, my hands are empty.
Listen, there is only wind in the tall grass,
        a throaty cry in the maples,
and these poor words, a trap for God,
a desperate prayer. *Eph'phatha*, be opened.
        Taking the deaf-mute aside,
he put his fingers into his ears, and then he spat
and touched his tongue with the spittle.
        Let the pain in. Push into it. Speak.

II

                      Long before sunrise,
        I steal out of the house
                and make my way to the cave
where they have put him, bringing spikenard as before,
                still in my nightdress,
                      my hair unbound,
        the wind gently in it, as once his hands,
                as once his voice, his warm breath.
As in the dream, the stone has been rolled away.
                I call his name
                      and stumble into the dark
        where we put him, and I find him nowhere
                in the rumpled sheets.
My Beloved has gone down to his garden,
                to his bed of spices,
                      I'm singing the words
        over and over, alone in the dark,

        to pasture his flock in the gardens
and gather lilies. Over and over, until I am empty and keen,
        I am my Beloved's
            and my Beloved is mine.
    And then into the emptiness,
        into the nowhere-here and hollowed
shell of the heart, sudden lightning, a bolt of morning—
        I'm dressed in a surge of sun
            in the wind's rising up
    with the day, in the rapture
one is breathed by—now the song singing *me*.
        My Beloved has gone down
            to his garden,
beyond the door of the cave, where the silhouettes
    I see are the voices of others
asking, *Where is he? Where have you put him?*
        And the song keeps on,
            the sun rising out of me,
    and the wind, and the garden
        of lilies, white and gold
and red as blood, his voice full in me, joined to my body,
        bright as the pollen in my hair.
        He is not here,
I call out, my hand on the stone.
        He is here, my hand on my throat,
but they flee from the tomb and say nothing to anyone,
        for they are afraid,
            they are sore afraid.

III

Could you not wait with me an hour?
    And so it is the betrayal, the denial,
the self-serving gift of myrrh to keep the body
    sweet—these touch me most.
How can I help it? Remember Nicodemus.
    How can I be born anew?

So frightened. So full of doubt. So fearful
    in the torchlit garden.

IV

                Not until I am standing before
the opened door, a great sky of stars
    exploding behind me,
and the beast of war in the cities and villages, the White Army
        ready to course over the steppes
           and into the hovel
where she has hidden with her children,
    do I know what to do.
"You must flee at once," I say. "You've been betrayed.
        They are coming to kill you."
           "How can I flee?"
She gestures—her children,
    too small.
"They won't look for you, I shall stay behind."
        "They will kill you."
           "Yes, but I have no children.
You must go." As I stop the story of her voice
    and try to see her,
I see first the rough-hewn hut, nearly bare, neither axe
        nor icon on the walls.
           What is darkness,
    that she should enter it?
        What is night, that she must
watch and wait an hour, two hours, two thousand years,
        before they come
           in the cold of the morning,
    the door brutally opened?
        She is alone in the dark,
she can leave, but she waits for the other woman's death
        to be enacted within her.
           And she is shot where she is,
    in a chair she has put not six feet

      from the door she knows will
open like a wound. I try to enter the mystery of her pain,
        able only to stand outside in the snow
          with the partisan
    whose heart is not fully ready
      to know what he has done.
Is it sorrow or guilt or holy joy that lets him see her,
       enthroned before him,
         in Rublev's flickering ocher
    and abstract blue, the golden
      child in her lap
naked and mortal and holy? The halo of a knothole
      blooms behind her.
        A girl of only sixteen years,
  who has not yet been with a man.

V

Can you not watch with me an hour? In St. Orain's,
    the morning I am to leave
the place of pilgrimage and song, I approach
    the plain brass cross
intending no word or vow, stunned to see
    my face in the polished surface,
in the cross of suffering and poverty and death
    my face, like a moon in water.
For just a moment I understand. One bare moment,
    the wind blowing through.
I put a small white stone from the deadyard there
    and go. *Are you Jesus?*
he was asked three times in the courtyard
    before the raging fire,
and with the cold of stone in his voice, three times
    he said, *No.*

ICON

I

To raise her spirits
someone has painted her toenails
with a lacquer clear as
the white of an egg but with flecks of glitter added in
to flash like mica,
like quartz in stone.
I have come a long way,
if the common measure of love
is loss, to rub her legs and her callused feet
with a lotion rich in lavender,
remembering how our mother
used to stand at the margin of our room, the door
narrowed open,
and sing into the dark where we lay unready for sleep,
an arbor of phosphorescent stars
pasted to the ceiling.
I don't know if the body believes the words
we offer it, or if it listens
only to the motive below the motive, octaves down—
but I still see her, about to withdraw,
and the stroke of light
that crossed the coverlet as her alto
patience and intimate
refrain lilted over us, like a hand stroking back
damp hair from a feverish forehead.
Side by side
in our twin beds, alone in the dark,
our small bodies
already ripening to the sweet danger within us—
to hear our mother sing to us
at the verge of limitless
night, the song offered up from the deep

                    harbor of her body,
must have gathered us, continued and carried us at rest
                    into the flushed, ready morning.
                                Ask me now
        if I believe in resurrection, body and mind—
                    I'd have to hum
what little I remember of the song that carried us
                    all through the night that was
                                deeper than we could know.
"I've named my left arm Lazarus," she confides,
                    and I nod,
letting my hands, wiser than I am, work the song
                    measure by measure into the muscles
                                of her left arm and leg.
"I see you," she says, turning her body slowly
                    toward the side of herself
she neglects, finding me there. *I see you*—said
                    without surprise or particular
                                emphasis, as if I hadn't,
        all these years, forgetting to remember her,
                    scorned and disregarded
part of my own heart. When finally I say, "See you
                    in the morning," she answers quickly,
                                "I'll be right here."

II

                                Alone in my own dark room,
        I lift my head from hands so wet
                    with tears they smell like rain
in a field of lavender. Afraid for her life, abandoned and to come,
                    I flip open my journal
                                and I see the words
            Do not fear. Only believe,
                    and she shall be well. Only believe.
Credo, it means give your heart, give it scorned and abandoned,
                    worthy and not worth much,

give it finally, freely.
What seems so far from you, I read,
is most your own.
I take the words into my body. Take them, sister,
into yours. They are light.
Or let me rub them lightly
on your skin, oil of lavender,
oil of rosemary and rue.
Alone in the body's dark nights, in its gardens and hovels,
in its rivers and mountains and many rooms,
together we lie down.

COMPLINE

    Seldom so intimate, night
  becomes wind in the deepest pool of the dark river,
like lilies the stars between my breasts, floating . . . and now
    I no longer want to sleep
  and the cup pass from me—flung out of my body
into yours, whoever you are, lean as the curve of a wing,
    the night your mantle,
  a blood rose blooming from your forehead—
as quietly a seam of clear sky opens, a motionless luster
    I'd call the moon of my birth month,
  were it not more likely the skin-thin huddle of linen
I left behind as I climbed up from the riverbank
    drenched in the darkness
  of the plunging center—sheets of fire, sheets of rain
on bare rock—and the jut of my hip bones
    felt as waves, waves
  cresting on the edge of cold air, a soundless
curl of white seen from a great height above the shore.

NIGHT-BLOOMING CEREUS

        Backlit by an endless field of night-blooming stars
                and ocean wind, each swelling bud
is suspended over an abyss of cool air,

        held in abeyance, not yet quite opened.
                Even so, the air
is a musk of readiness that draws us

        bodily to the fipple hole of one stout bud,
                and we sit down together
before this omphalos in a kind of trance—

        more than ordinary waiting, we've been summoned,
                the scent so stirring, so supple
it's an oil applied to our skin

        by a kneeling woman's rich spill of night silk hair.
                As we wait, I study the bud,
prodigal on its crook of stem,

        notched or mortised to the edge of its leaf,
                and I try to map its beginnings,
following back along the rib that diverged

        from a slender channel drawn down the middle
                of its succulent splay—
as if in search of the green fuse,

        as if I might locate the source
                of all blossoming, as if by wanting to
I might trip the fine coiled spring

        at the invisible center, and listen to
                the silent waterfall *whoo-ree*
that begins the gradual whorl of inflorescence.

Who knows how opening opens, how suffering
        suffers, how love finds itself
in love. . . . Without asking,

    I ask it, and a long, fluted sepal springs lightly free
        of the bundled embrace the bud is
and trembles in the air, one finger

    in silence lifted. And now the wheel we can't see
        shudders somewhere
within the tinder of the Void,

    flinging off in a fimbriate blaze new comets and stars—
        and in the all-inclusive key
of no sound all harmony the cereus

    breath by breath gathers all of night and ocean
        and the falling flower of the moon
into its deep heart . . . and hovers open.

HYMN TO NIGHT

I

Wanting to touch
the night within me to the night out there, I let night
be a stone,
the stone I keep under my pillow,
part salt and thunder,
part moon and white-capped wave thrust through
black magma.
Tongue the stone, taste the ocean—
the waves keep coming in, coming in
as if sounding the depths, as if trying to sense beneath
sea floor and earth's crust,
radiant and roiling, the dark forge that fuses
light and dark together
on a single wick—a thrumming force that has no fury in it,
no forgiveness, no
idea of union. Listen, whoever you are
soaked dark with love sweat,
it is good to be unable to sleep at night. Bring your face
closer, let's move at rest
into the boundless tide-gate night, beyond
blessed or *dreadful*, as if listening
for God, and be the lilt of the pine boughs as wind
lifts and lets go,
lifts and lets go, until there is nothing left
outside our breathing,
and the rain gives way to a torrent of stars, and the moon,
rising out of the wind, rivers here
in the shining shadow night is.

II

                And the stone is
also the black core, a pivot set before me at day's end,
                      the perihelion
        on which I turn and burn,
                stripped down, simplified
to intimate refrain. Soon or late, night finds us
                  here alone—
selfwrung, selfstrung, self in self steeped—
        or sprung past turbulence,
past stalling, taking wing, daring anything, allowed
                in deep innerness
      to bank and soar—as over the night sea
              the fulmar, spiraling
like a lariat, dives in sheer dare, headlong—then rises,
                borne along
      on a wing of the wind, its inner icon
            a star wheel, turning.
Tonight, at rest in the dark, unafraid, simply one of the winds
                in the hymn thrum
    that begins with the flute of the wood thrush
          at dusk, tell me,
you who are the breath within the breath, is it you I spend
              my whole life
     loving? Through the nightbook borderland
          starbank window now
only the wind whispers itself, *No holiness, vast emptiness,* no
            word on the bright mirror
     snow nimbus moth orchid
        moon, shorn and full—
just this wind as it ferries round *no one, alone* to *all one,*
           a star-knot of oaks and oceans,
      great heart, wheel, and bone.

NOTES

IONA CANTICLE

The poem incorporates Gaelic names for places on the island of Iona, where word and place are knit together by history and usage. The following list gives the words in the order that they appear in the poem, with attention to how they are pronounced on Iona.

> Caolas Annraidh (Cal-la-*nu*-rah): Strait of the Storm, located at the north tip of the island
> traigh mor (tray-more): big shore, located at the southeast of the island
> cnoc (crock): hill
> carraig (*kah*-rig): rock
> machair (*mack*er): grassland along the west of Iona at the Bay at the Back of the Ocean
> Port a'Churaich (Port ah *Cu*rrick): Port of the Coracle. A bay at the southern tip of Iona where Columcille landed in 563
> Port Beul Mor (Port Bull More): small beach on the southwest shore of Iona
> Anmchara (Ah-nam-*ka*-ra): soul friend, spiritual advisor
> Reilig Orain (*Rell*-ig *Ore*-ran): St. Oran's graveyard
> I mo chridhe (Ee-mah-cree): Iona of my love
> I mo ghraidh (Ee-mah-gree): Iona of my heart

HOUSE OF STONE AND SONG

Blessed are the single ones . . . The lines come from the Gospel According to St. Thomas.

ICON (*"That man standing there, who is he?"*)

This poem incorporates words and lines in translation from Goethe, Pablo Neruda, Zbigniew Herbert, and Paul Celan.

COLLECT ("Autumn wind scatters . . .")

Prayers are not enough. You must do something. A line from Rumi, as translated by Coleman Barks

STRANGE ALTARS
The verse that begins the poem is from the Kena Upanishad.

AT DÚN DÚCHATHAIR
When I returned from Aran, I read Tim Robinson's masterful book *Stones of Aran: Pilgrimage*, from which the information in the epigraph is taken almost verbatim. For more about Mícheál Ó Maolláin of Baile na Creige and the cliffmen, see "The Cliffman's Kingdom" in Robinson's book. The Gaelic words below appear in the order that they appear in the poem.

> barr aille (bawr *awl*-yeh): top of the cliffs
> creachoileán (crack-ill*aun*): island of woe. Derived from creach (ruination) and oileán (island)
> Is mór an trua: What a pity; How sad it is
> seanchaí (*shan*-a-kee): storyteller, old poet
> carraig an: rock of
> ailleadóir (alyeh-dore): cliffman
> Árainn: Aran, the largest island of the Aran Island group, which comprises Inis Oírr, Inis Meáin, and Árainn. The Anglicized names for the islands are Inisheer, Inishmaan, and Inishmore.

REQUIEM: A POEM IN FIVE VOICES
The five speakers in the poem are not intended to represent specific people. The voices are fictional, although the drownings are not. The first speaker is a father of one of the drowned boys; the second is a textile artist and weaver; the third is a mother of one of the boys; the fourth is one of the drowned; the last is another mother. The Gaelic and Scots words below are listed in the order in which they appear in the poem.

> machair (*mack*er): a stretch of grassland along the Bay at the Back of the Ocean
> strath: valley
> hirst: a barren piece of land
> smoored: damped down
> hint: at the back of, or rear
>
> Tigh na Bearg (Gaelic): House of the Weaving
> harled: roughcast with lime and small stones

snowcemmed: whitewashed
hettle: fishermen's name for the rough, stony sea bottom some distance from the shore
port-a-beul (porshta*bee*al): a fast tune to which sounds are added to make it easier to sing when the words aren't exactly known; or "mouth music," offered in the absence of instrumental accompaniment
stravaiging (stra*vaig*ing): roaming, wandering aimlessly
lochan: a small lake

kailyard: a garden of kale
clachan: a small village
gowl: a howling gust of wind
(During the Clearances, many Highlanders were turned out of their crofts and villages, moved to stony ground or made to emigrate. Some of the ships used for their transport were refitted from the slave trade. *On the Crofter's Trail: In Search of the Clearance Highlanders* by David Craig is the primary source of information for this part of "Requiem.")

ben: inwards, inner part; to claim one's ben is to find one's rightful place
hoise: to raise or heave up
stour: strife

dinnle: vibration of thunder or of bells; to tingle with cold or with pain
displenished: stripped of furnishing or of stock
glotten: partly thawed
glet: filth, mucus, slime
deliverance: a formal decision or judgment
skewl (skee*ool*): to turn aside or twist
dirl: pain caused by a blow
How the word hurts: The words echo those of Peter Matthiessen's character Mr. Watson at the conclusion of *Bone by Bone*.

TENEBRAE

The title is Latin plural for darkness, shadows—and the name for the service of matins and lauds in the last three days of Holy Week, commemorating the suffering and death of Jesus. At the close of the ceremony, there is a resounding moment, called *strepitus,* when the monks in unison close their books of chants, after which they remain in silent meditation in the dark room. Part IV is in part based on a story told about a Russian woman named Natalie in *The Essence of Prayer* by Metropolitan Anthony of Sourozh.

HYMN TO NIGHT

No holiness, vast emptiness. These words were uttered by the First Chinese Patriarch Bodhidharma, when asked by Emperor Wu, "Then what is the primary meaning of the holy truth?"